Cooking
making things to eat

A Puffin Book
Written and produced by McPhee Gribble Publishers
Illustrated by David Lancashire
Copyright © Penguin Books Australia Ltd, 1976

About cooking

Cooking is the way people turn raw food into things that look and taste different and sometimes better.

Heat is most often used to alter raw food. Other foods are just changed by the way they are mixed together. Cold can be used sometimes too.

There is no one way to cook. All over the world people have worked out different things to do with food that taste good.

Ways of cooking have been slowly discovered by people trying out new ideas, changing the amounts in mixtures, and sometimes inventing another good thing to eat by accident.

You can change food yourself by adding some of your own ideas. Add small amounts at a time and taste the food as you go.

If you have the space see if you can make a cooking place outside.

All you need are a work bench, some cooking gear and a safe fireplace.

Collect several old saucepans, a frying pan, some containers, spoons, a knife and a fork.

Have a bucket of water to throw on the fire when you have finished cooking. Use it to soak dirty pots and pans in too.

Cooking inside is best kept simple. Get everything out that you will need before you start.

Spread lots of newspaper around so you can bundle up the mess at the end.

An oven takes a while to heat up – so turn it on before you begin.

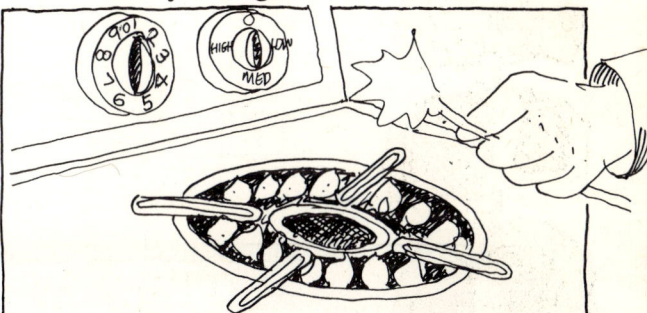

If the stove you are using is a gas stove, turn the oven or hot plate knob to the right number and very quickly light the gas.

An electric stove just needs turning on to the temperature your food needs.

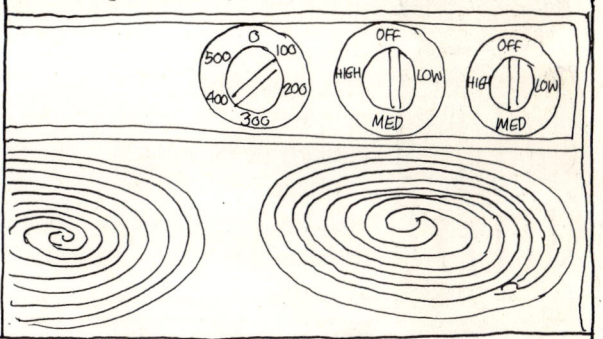

While you are cooking check that the heat isn't too high. If a pan is bubbling fast turn the heat down a bit. Ovens can be turned down towards the end of the cooking time if your food looks too brown.

Shishkebabs

these are also called shashlick

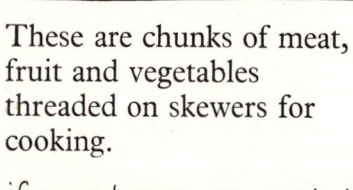

These are chunks of meat, fruit and vegetables threaded on skewers for cooking.

if you have no metal skewers ask a butcher for wooden ones — or use very long clean nails

All kinds of food can be cut into cubes for shishkebabs. Choose several different things to thread on.

Any of these are good.
Lamb, beef, bacon or sausage
apple
onion
tomato
green pepper
prunes
cooked potato
cabbage
zucchini (courgettes)
mushrooms
apricots
marshmallows

Chop the meat into cubes about this size with a sharp knife. If you use bacon, cut each rasher into 4 pieces and roll them up.

Chop all the fruit and vegetables you choose into chunks like the meat.

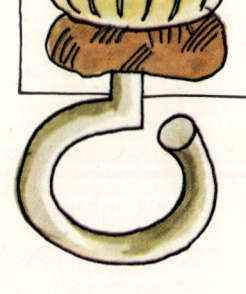

scrape out seeds

Thread the different chunks onto the skewers so the flavours mix. Put soft things next to crunchy things.

pack them tightly and sprinkle with salt and pepper

they are now ready to cook

Shishkebabs can be grilled, cooked on a barbecue or fried.

If you grill them turn the griller on to the highest heat.

Put the shishkebabs on the grill pan or on the top of the barbecue. A few knobs of butter or margarine, or a dribble of oil on them will stop them getting too dry.

Turn them every 5 minutes.

If you want to fry them instead, choose a frying pan that the skewers will fit into.

The gas or electricity under the hotplate should be turned on to medium heat.

Melt a spoon of oil or butter in the pan before you put in the shishkebabs.

hot

Turn the skewers over every 5 minutes with a fork. The shishkebabs are cooked when the meat is brown and crisp at the edges.

You take them off the skewers before you eat them.

Hold the end of the skewer and gently push the chunks down on to your plate with a fork. Don't push too hard or they will go everywhere.

Shishkebabs are good with salad or wrapped in a piece of bread or roll.

Chocolate balls

You will need half a cup of each of these
- coconut
- sugar
- butter cut in small chunks
- cocoa
- milk
- 2 big cups of rolled oats, muesli or granola
- other things can go in – like sultanas, chopped fruit or nuts

Put the butter, sugar and milk in a large pan and stir them over a low heat until the sugar melts.

Tip everything else in and mix them together well.

Leave the mixture for about half an hour in a cool place to set.

Now shape the chocolate balls. You can roll them in more coconut or nuts if you like.

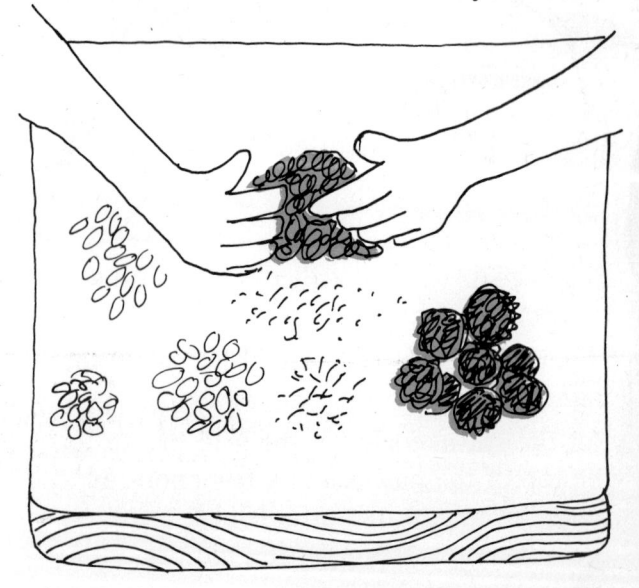

Leave them to set again for a while.

Jelly sweets
a quick kind of Turkish Delight

You will need
- a packet of jelly
- ½ a cup of a mixture of icing sugar and cornflour
- some chopped nuts if you like

Follow the instructions for making jelly on the packet but use only half the water. This makes a very strong jelly.

Stir in chopped nuts now if you have them.

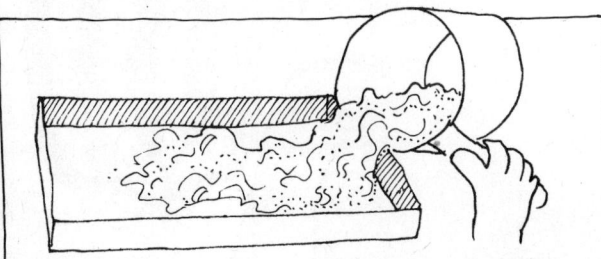

Pour the jelly into a small flat pan and leave it to set.

Cut the jelly into squares and loosen them with an egg slice.

Roll the sweets in lots of the cornflour and icing sugar on a plate.

they get sticky so eat them now

Biscuit cake

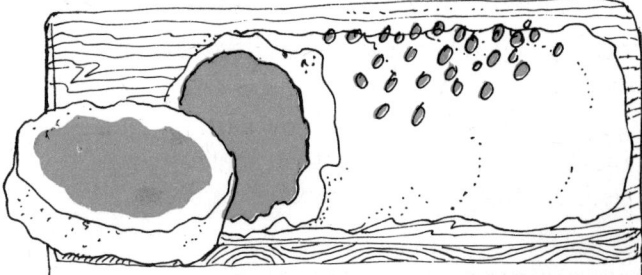

This is an almost instant cake. All you need are about 12 plain sweet biscuits – ginger or chocolate are good – and a large cup of cream.

Beat the cream in a bowl until it is very stiff.

Now stick all the biscuits together with cream and stand them on their sides on a plate. Cover the roll with cream too.

Sprinkle the roll with nuts or chopped dried fruit – anything you feel like.

Put it in the fridge for a few hours to make the biscuits soggy with cream.

Stuffed things

Fruit or vegetables can be stuffed with a mixture you can invent.

Choose a kind you can hollow out. Tomatoes, peppers, eggplant, marrow, a whole cabbage, apples, peaches, apricots work well.

Make a sweet or meaty mixture to stuff them with.

If you want a sweet stuffing try things like dried fruit and nuts mixed with sugar, a few slices of butter or pieces of chocolate.

Minced meat mixed with an egg, some grated onion, salt and pepper is good. Try canned fish or chunks of cheese with grated onion.

A sweet mixture in vegetables or a meaty mixture in fruit can be good too.

The stuffing should feel fairly dry. The juice from the fruit or vegetable oozes into it as it cooks. Stir in a little bread or cereal if the stuffing is very sticky.

Scrape out the middle of the thing to be stuffed with a sharp knife and a spoon. Get rid of seeds and make a deep hollow for the stuffing.

Stuffed things can be cooked in a pan with a tight lid. Pour in about a cup of juice or water. Cook them slowly over a low heat.

Or they can go in a dish in a medium hot oven with a little butter and water around them.

Cook them until the stuffed things are tender.

Soft cheese

This is the easiest kind of cheese to make and has been made in many parts of the world for hundreds of years.

You will need
- 1 litre of milk
- 1 junket tablet
- 1 teaspoon of salt
- a coarse clean cloth (like an old tea towel)
- a saucepan, a spoon and two bowls

Put the milk in the saucepan over a low heat until it is lukewarm.

Crush the junket tablet in a bowl with the back of a spoon. Now dissolve the tablet in a few spoons of cold water.

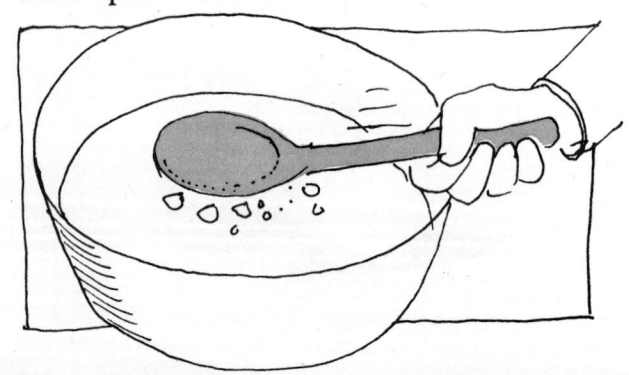

Pour the milk into the same bowl and stir.

Leave it to set in a warm place. In about 15 minutes the rennet from the tablet will clot the protein in the milk into a thick curd and a watery whey.

Cut the surface of the junket crisscross with the spoon and stir in the salt.

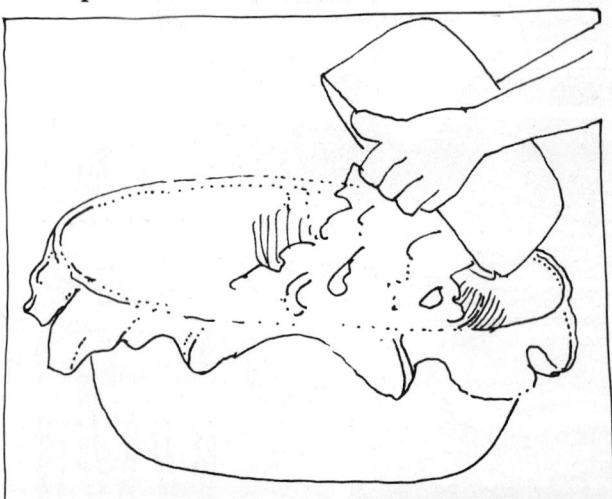

Now put your cloth over the other basin and pour the junket into it.

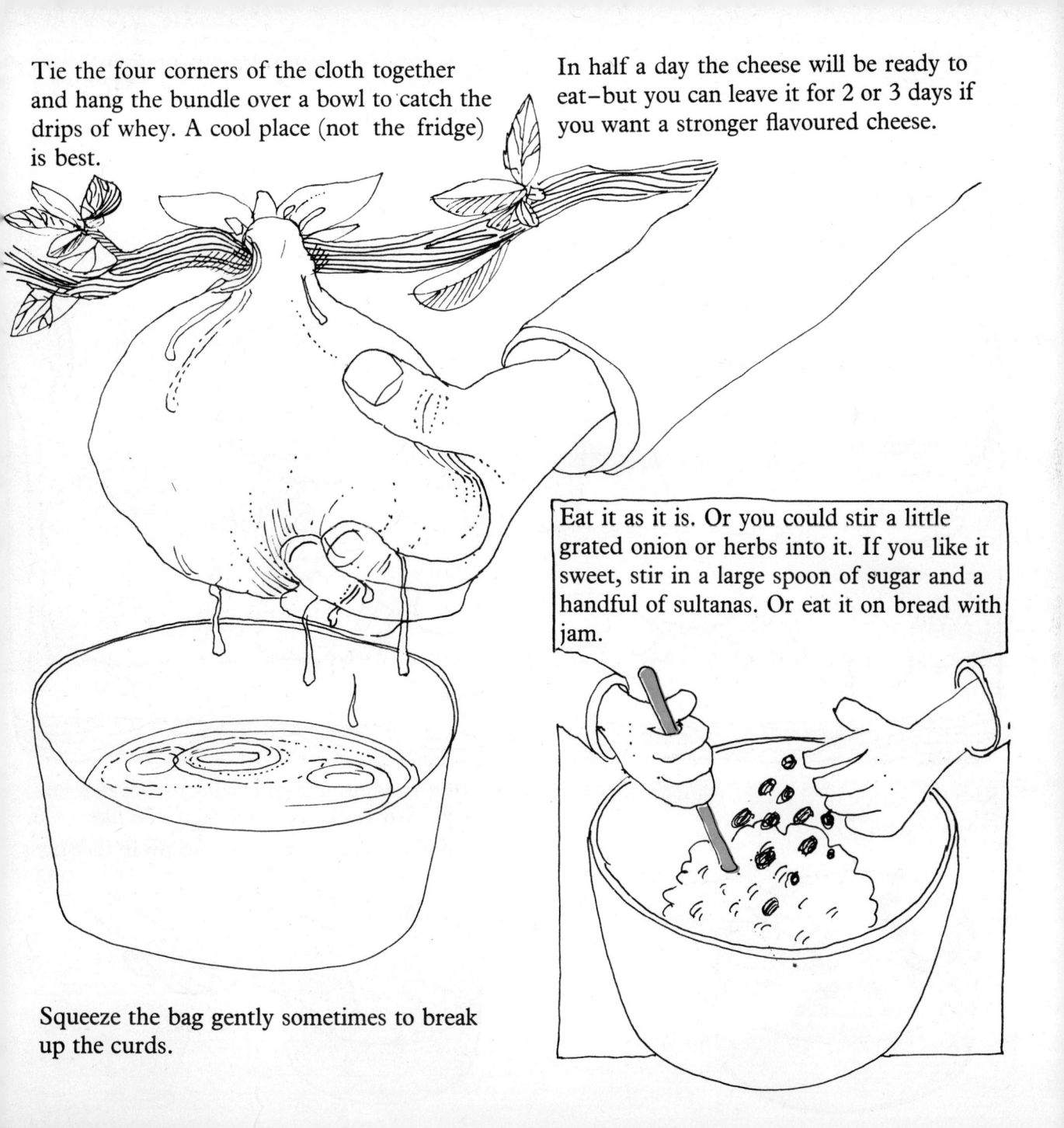

Tie the four corners of the cloth together and hang the bundle over a bowl to catch the drips of whey. A cool place (not the fridge) is best.

In half a day the cheese will be ready to eat – but you can leave it for 2 or 3 days if you want a stronger flavoured cheese.

Eat it as it is. Or you could stir a little grated onion or herbs into it. If you like it sweet, stir in a large spoon of sugar and a handful of sultanas. Or eat it on bread with jam.

Squeeze the bag gently sometimes to break up the curds.

Cakes

This is enough for a big cake or about 15 little cakes.

Turn the oven on before you begin. 350 degrees for an electric stove or mark 4 for a gas stove – light it quickly.

① Collect everything together first.

Any of these flavourings are good or make up your own.

a few drops of vanilla
2 tablespoons of cocoa
a handful of currants or sultanas
a mashed banana
a grated apple
orange juice and grated peel – leave out half the milk

- an almost full cup of sugar
- a heaped cup of self-raising flour
- ½ a cup of milk
- a large saucepan and a wooden spoon
- a cake tin or paper cases
- 2 eggs
- 2 tablespoons of butter

② Rub the inside of the cake tin with butter or oil on a scrap of paper.

③ Melt the butter in the saucepan over a low heat. Stir in the cocoa now if you like.

Take the pan off the heat and tip in the sugar.

4) Break in the eggs and stir well. Then the flour and flavouring if you have some.

5) Now slowly add the milk or juice stirring all the time.

6) Keep stirring until the mixture is smooth and shiny. Lumps can be beaten out with an egg beater.

7) Now pour the mixture into the cake tin. Or put large spoonfuls into the paper cases.

8) Put the cake or cakes into the middle of the oven and shut the door very quickly. A large cake will take about 40 minutes to cook and small cakes about 25 minutes.

All ovens are different so your cakes may take more or less time. Don't open the door until about 5 minutes before they should be cooked. Cold air makes the cakes sink.

Stick a fork into the centre – it should come out clean and dry if the cake is cooked right through.

9) Cool the cake on something that lets the air in underneath. The wire rack out of a griller pan will do.

Loosen the cake with a knife and turn it out on to the rack. Small cakes stay in the paper cases.

Let the cake get quite cold before you ice and decorate it – or eat it hot.

Things sometimes go wrong with cakes but they still taste good. Cut off burnt bits and cover soggy parts with jam or ice cream.

Dumplings also called Knodel

These are balls of dough cooked in a juicy sauce. As dumplings cook they swell to twice their size.

They are good things to cook outside over a fire. You will need a large old saucepan with a tight lid.

Dumplings can be cooked in a sweet sauce or a meaty mixture.

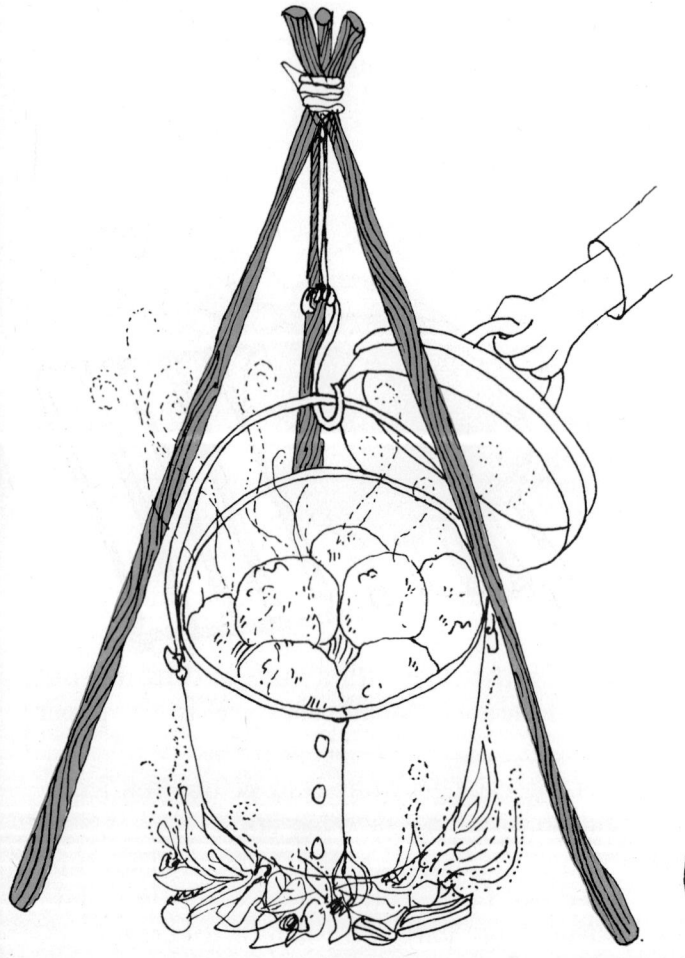

Make a sauce to cook them in. Try dumplings cooked in canned soup or stew.

An extra cup of water should be stirred into stew to make it juicy enough.

For sweet dumplings put this collection of things into the saucepan.
- 1 cup of water
- ½ a cup of sugar
- 1 large spoon of syrup or honey
- a large lump of butter

Now make the dough. This makes 6 big dumplings to feed 3 people.

You will need
- 1 cup of self-raising flour
- 1 tablespoon of butter cut in small bits
- 1 egg
- 2 or 3 tablespoons of milk

Put the flour in a large bowl with the butter.

Rub the butter into the flour with dry fingers. Keep rubbing until you can't feel the butter and the mixture is fine and crumbly.

Make a hollow and break in the egg. Mix it in with a fork or your hand.

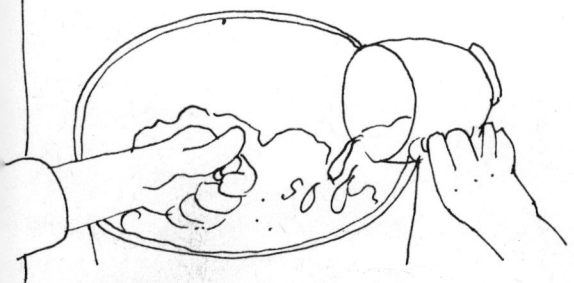

Add the milk a little at a time – until the dough will press together into a ball. If it gets too wet sprinkle in more flour.

Try not to squash all the air out of the dough – handle it gently.

Make the dough into a long roll and cut it into 6 pieces. Pat them gently into balls.

Now put the pan of sauce over a medium heat until it boils. Then gently lower the dough balls in with a spoon.

Put the lid on the pan. Turn down the heat now – so the sauce is just bubbling quietly.

The dumplings will be ready in 20 minutes.

Flowers and leaves

Some flowers and leaves can be eaten like sweets or used for decorating things.

You give them a sugary coating and crisp them very slowly in the oven.

Choose a collection of some of these – they are safe to eat.

parsley
mint leaves
nasturtium petals
violets
rose petals

Don't eat any other flowers or leaves – some are poisonous.

You will need
- a small clean paint brush
- an egg white
- castor sugar
- some leaves and flowers

Stir the egg white with a fork for a few moments.

Dry the leaves and flowers gently with a paper tissue.

Coat them with the paint brush dipped in egg white. Then sprinkle each one with castor sugar.

Notice spots where the sugar won't stick and dab on more egg white. The sugar should cover them well.

Turn the oven on to its lowest heat. Put the sugared flowers and leaves on a sheet of waxed paper or foil.
Leave the oven door half open. The sugared things should be left to dry right out – overnight is best.

Store the dry flowers and leaves in an airtight container until you want them.

Bread

This is one of the oldest foods and one of the best things to make. It is not as hard as it sounds.

Bread takes about 3 hours from start to finish – but you can do other things while it rises.

To make 1 loaf you will need

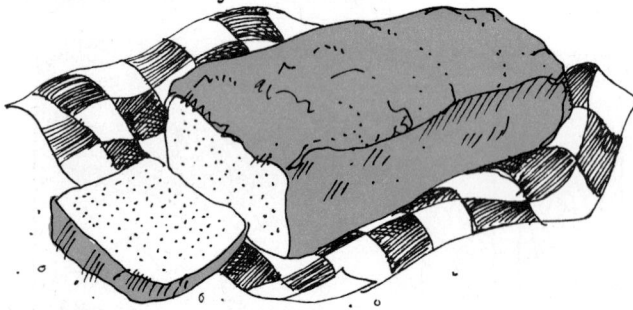

- 3 cups of flour – this can be plain, wholemeal, or a mixture of both
- 1 tablespoon of fresh yeast or 2 teaspoons of dried yeast
- 1 cup of warm water – not hot
- 1 teaspoon of sugar
- 1 teaspoon of salt

Get these things ready as well.

YEAST

Yeast is the magic ingredient in bread which makes it rise and feel light. Yeast is a plant. It needs warmth, food – sugar and flour – and water to grow.

You can use fresh yeast which looks like putty, or dried yeast from a packet.

There are 2 very important things to do when you are making bread. First knead the dough for a long time to mix the yeast through. Then have a warm place to leave it to rise – in the sun or by a warm stove perhaps.

Kneading is a special way of mixing dough with your hands. It is hard work. The dough will slowly change from a sticky mess into a smooth springy lump. Keep 1 cup of the flour you need for sprinkling on your hands and the dough while you work.

large bowl
small bowl
cup
clean cloth
floury board
baking tin rubbed with butter or oil

1. mix yeast with ½ a cup of warm water and a spoon of sugar

2. put 2 cups of flour and a spoon of salt into bowl — make a well with your fist

3. pour in yeast and sprinkle with flour — leave in a warm place until the yeast froths

4. pour in ½ a cup of warm water — mix very well with floury hands into a smooth lump

5. cover with cloth and leave in a warm place — after about 45 minutes the dough will be twice as big

6. turn dough on to a floury board — with very floury hands knead the dough until your wrists ache — then some more

7. turn the oven on to 450 degrees or gas mark 8 to heat up — shape the dough into a loaf in the tin — leave it to rise to the top for another 45 minutes

8. put the loaf in the oven — after 10 minutes turn the oven down to 350 degrees or gas mark 4

9. have a look after 45 minutes — the loaf is cooked when it shakes out of the tin and sounds hollow when you tap it

Jam

Jam is what you get when fruit and some vegetables are boiled with the right amount of sugar.

Different fruits and vegetables are cooked in different ways to make jam.

Here are 2 kinds of jam you could make with a small amount of fruit. You will get 2 small jars of jam.

Apple jam

You will need
- 3 large apples or 5 small ones
- 1 cup of light brown sugar
- ½ a cup of water
- the grated peel and juice from ½ an orange or lemon

Peel and core the apples and cut them into slices.

Put the sliced apples in a large pan with a lid. Add the water and the grated peel and juice.

Cook the apples over a low heat until they are soft. This takes about 10 minutes.

Tip in the sugar and stir until it melts.

Now leave the lid off and turn the heat up a little. The mixture will start to bubble gently all over.

Stir it now and then to make sure it isn't sticking. Turn the heat down a bit if it is.

Warm 2 small very clean jars now – in hot water or a low oven.

When the mixture has been bubbling for 15 minutes test it to see if jelly is forming.

TEST AND BOTTLE

Drop a spoon of juice on to a cold saucer. If a thick skin forms when the juice cools the jam is ready. Keep testing every few minutes until it is right.

Now use a cup to scoop the jam into the jars. It will be very hot – so stand the jars on a damp cloth to stop them cracking.

While the jam is still hot cover the jars tightly – with a screw top or plastic food wrap and rubber bands.

Raspberry jam

you can use loganberries or mulberries for this jam too

You need the same weight of fruit and sugar for this jam.

Wash the raspberries and put them in a saucepan. Squash them a bit so that some of the juice runs out.

Boil the fruit over a medium heat for 3 minutes.

Tip in the sugar and boil the mixture for 8 minutes.

Stir the jam often or it can stick and burn.

Pancakes

This will make 4 big pancakes about the size of dinner plates or lots of small ones.

You will need
- 1 cup plain flour
- 1 egg
- 1 cup of milk
- ½ teaspoon of salt
- butter or oil for frying
- a large mixing bowl, a frying pan, a spoon, an egg slice and a cup

Large pancakes can have a filling. Soft fruit, cream cheese and sultanas, or grated cheese and tomato are a few ideas. You will need about 2 big spoonfuls of filling for each pancake. A sprinkle of sugar and lemon juice is good too.

Put flour and salt in the bowl and break in the egg. Start stirring and add the milk very slowly. You might not need it at all.

Stir until the lumps are gone and the mixture runs off the spoon like thin cream. This is the batter.

Put the frying pan on the hot plate turned to medium heat. Leave the pan for a few minutes to get really hot.

Melt a small lump of butter or a teaspoon of oil in the pan.

For big pancakes pour in about ½ a cup of batter and tilt the pan until the bottom is thinly covered.

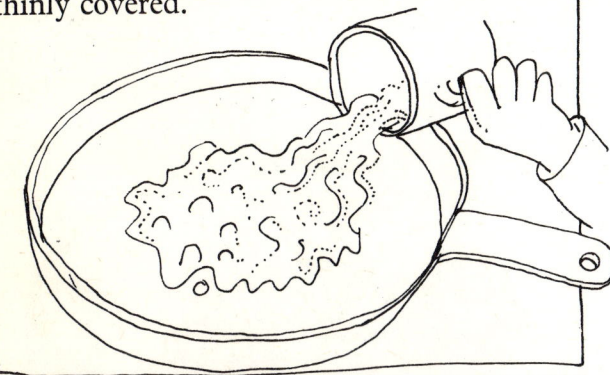

For small pancakes put in spoonfuls of batter. Leave space between them as they spread.

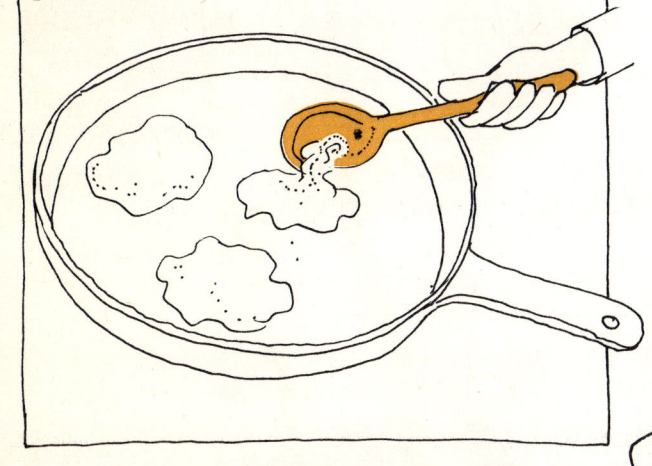

You should see air bubbles come to the surface as the first side is nearly cooked.

Small pancakes cook quite fast. Put in more butter or oil for each panful.

Lift up a corner of a large pancake and check that it is golden brown. Then turn it over with the egg slice.

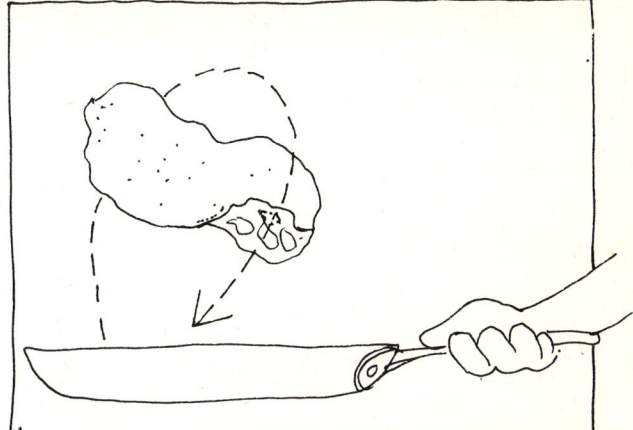

Or try tossing it to turn it over – but be prepared to eat a dirty pancake.

While the second side is cooking spread your filling on or sprinkle sugar and lemon. Roll the pancake up and slide it out of the pan with the egg slice.

Now put in more butter or oil and start again.

If you are making pancakes for more than 1 person, you can turn the oven on to the lowest heat, and keep the pancakes hot on a plate.

Foodburgers

You will need
- 1 egg
- 1 cup of minced meat or fish
- ½ cup of cereal (like cornflakes, porridge, cooked rice)
- 1 teaspoon of salt
- 6 shakes of pepper
- 1 large spoon of fat or oil
- ½ cup of your own ideas
  a mixture of some of these is good – raisins, grated onion or apple, nuts or peanut butter, chutney, tomato sauce, chopped bacon, baked beans, any cooked vegetables chopped small

Mix everything with your hands in a large bowl.

Try to make 2 firm balls with the mixture. If it feels too wet add more cereal – if too dry and crumbly add a little milk or tomato sauce.

Put the pan on the hotplate turned to medium heat. Then drop in a spoonful of fat or oil.

Carefully put in the burger balls and flatten them a bit with a fork.

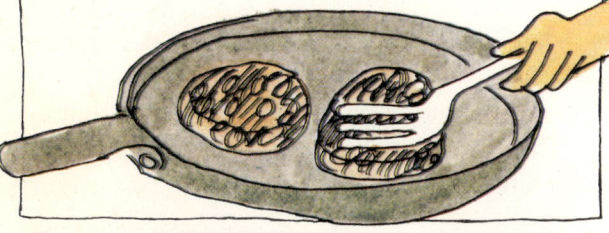

Turn the burgers over after 5 minutes. They should be brown and crisp looking.

If you are very hungry, put a slice of bacon into the pan now, and break in an egg.

Turn the bacon after 3 minutes and the burgers again if they are not brown enough.

Make 4 slices of toast or split 2 bread rolls in half.

Slices of tomato, potato crisps, lettuce and tomato sauce can go in the foodburger too. Pile everything you choose in layers with the burger in the middle.

Ice cream

Your own ice cream is twice as good as shop ice cream.

You will need
- 2 eggs
- ½ a cup of cream
- 2 tablespoons of icing sugar

First separate the egg yolks from the egg whites. This is rather hard to do. You want the yolks in a cup and the whites in a mixing bowl.

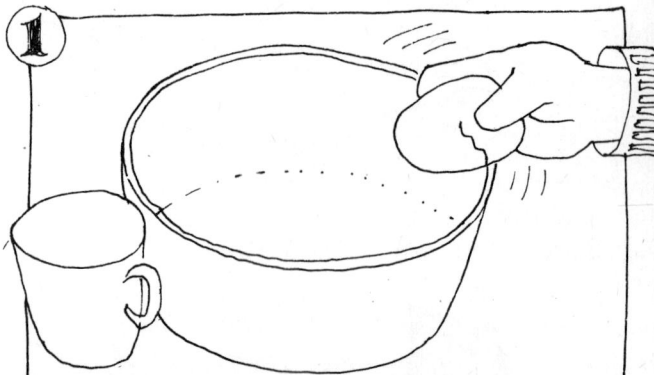

1. Crack the egg on the edge of the bowl and gently break the shell into 2 halves with your fingers.

2. Tip the yolk carefully from one shell half to the other, and back again. The white dribbles down into the bowl.

3 Beat the egg whites with an egg beater until they make a thick white froth.

In another bowl beat the cream until it is thick. Two people could share the beating.

4 Tip the cream into the egg whites and mix them together well.

5 Put the egg yolks into the empty bowl and tip in the sugar. Stir into a smooth mixture.

6 Mix everything together. Flavour the ice cream now if you like. Try peanut butter or small pieces of fruit.

7 Pour the mixture into a small cake tin or ice tray and put it in the freezer.

The ice cream will take an hour or so to freeze hard.

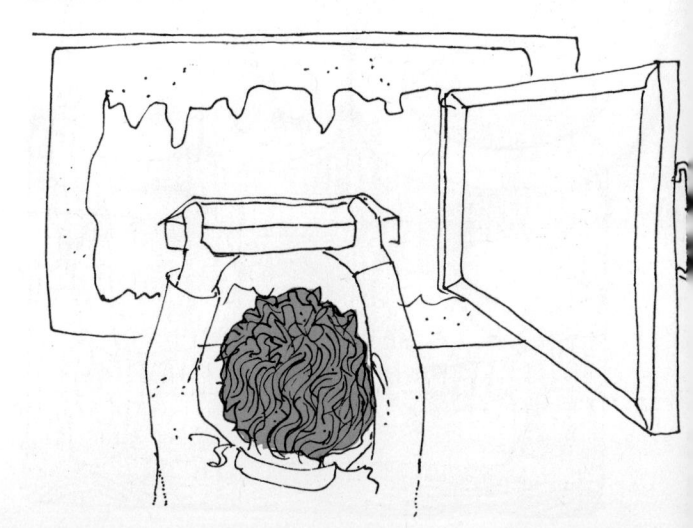

Fruit tart

This is a pie without a lid that is filled with a juicy fruit mixture.

Canned or fresh fruit can be used for the filling sprinkled with a little sugar and knobs of butter.

You can buy pastry ready to roll out. Shortcrust pastry works best for pies. If the pastry is frozen or very hard leave it to soften.

Get everything ready before you start.

Turn the oven on to 400 degrees or gas mark 6. Light the gas quickly and carefully.

You will need
- half a packet of shortcrust pastry
- a little flour for sprinkling
- fruit, sugar and butter
- a rolling pin
- a pie plate or 2 old saucers
- a sharp knife

Sprinkle a little flour on a flat surface. Keep your hands and the rolling pin floury too. Pastry gets sticky if you don't. Add more flour as you roll.

Roll out the pastry. Turn it around between rollings to keep it the right shape.

Roll it until the pastry is bigger than your pie plate or big enough to cut in half for 2 saucers.

Leave the pastry on the bench to settle its shape while you prepare the filling.

If you are using canned fruit drain off the syrup. Slice fresh fruit – there is no need to peel most kinds. Put in a few nuts, sultanas or a few spoons of jam if you like.

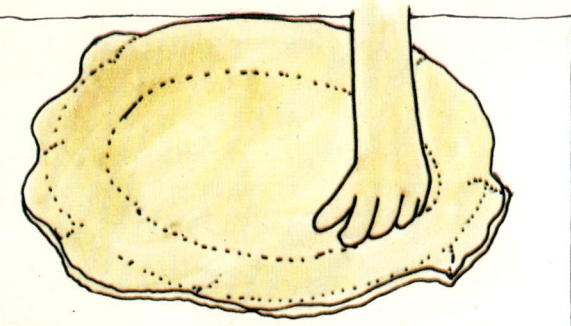

Now lift the pastry into the dish. It must fit without stretching – it shrinks a little when it cooks. Press it into corners gently with your knuckles.

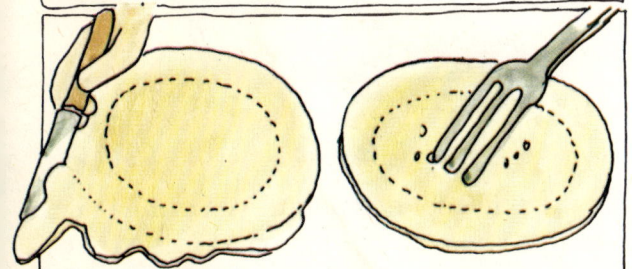

Trim around the edge with a knife.
Prick holes all over the bottom of the tart with a fork.

Put in the fruit filling. If your dish is a deep one make several layers of fruit sprinkled with sugar and knobs of butter.
Finish the top with more sugar and butter.

Press around the edge with the back of a fork.

You could use spare strips of pastry to decorate the tart if you like.

Cook it in the centre of the oven for about half an hour. Look at it before then to check that the edge isn't cooking too fast. Turn the oven down a bit if the edge looks burnt.

Potato egg

This is a potato cooked in its jacket and eaten like a boiled egg.

Heat up the oven before you start. An electric oven should be turned on to about 400 degrees. A gas oven should be turned to mark 6 – light it very carefully and quickly.

Or you could wrap the potato in 3 or 4 thicknesses of foil and put it in the fire (not the hottest part or it will burn).

Choose a potato the size you could eat – an egg-shaped one works best.

Wash the skin well and dry it, then prick it several times with a fork. Smear the potato all over with a little butter or margarine on a scrap of paper.

Put the potato on a rack in the centre of the oven. Test it after 45 minutes but if the potato is a big one it will take about an hour to cook. 2 small ones take ½ an hour

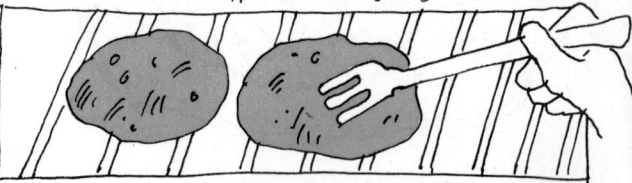

The potato is cooked when a fork goes into the centre easily. Use a cloth to take it out of the oven.

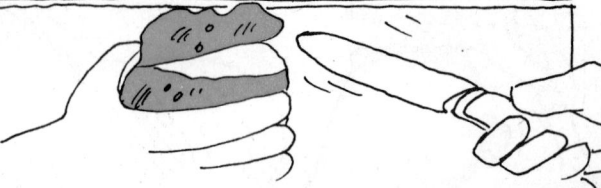

Let the skin cool down until you can handle it easily. Then cut the top off as if it were a boiled egg.

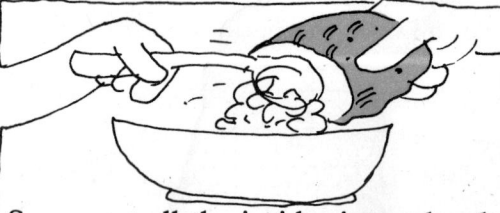

Scoop out all the insides into a bowl. Add a spoon of butter or margarine, a pinch of salt and a few shakes of pepper. Mash it all well with a fork and keep tasting until it is right for you. Chopped parsley or grated onion is good too.

Spoon the mixture back into the potato skin and put the lid on.
Eat it with a spoon.

Mumbled eggs

This is enough for one person. Double everything for two.

Mumbled eggs are even nicer than scrambled eggs. They are very quick to make and perfect for a breakfast in bed for someone.

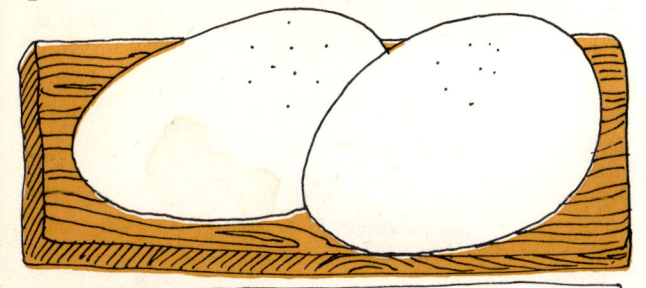

All you need are
- 2 eggs
- 1 large teaspoon of butter or margarine
- salt and pepper
- a frying pan or a small saucepan
- a fork

Melt the butter in the pan and break in the eggs. The hotplate should be turned to medium heat.

Add a pinch of salt and 3 or 4 shakes of pepper.

Stir gently with a fork until the eggs start to thicken.

Take the pan off the heat and keep stirring. The heat of the pan will finish cooking the eggs.

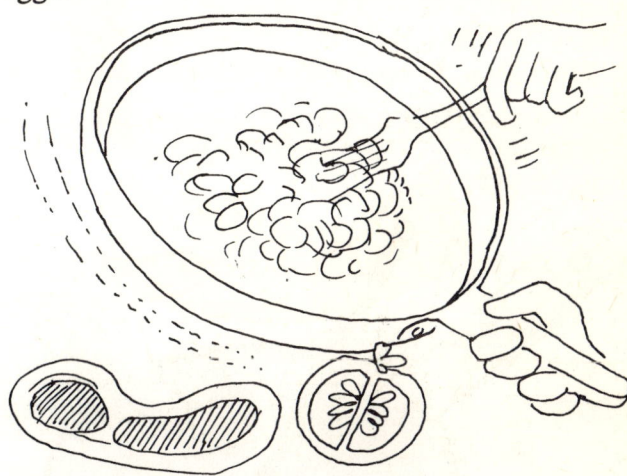

Other things can be added if you like. Before you break in the eggs, you could put in some small pieces of bacon or tomato. Or you could leave out the salt and pepper and make sweet mumbled eggs. For this you just add a spoon of sugar and a small handful of sultanas at the end.

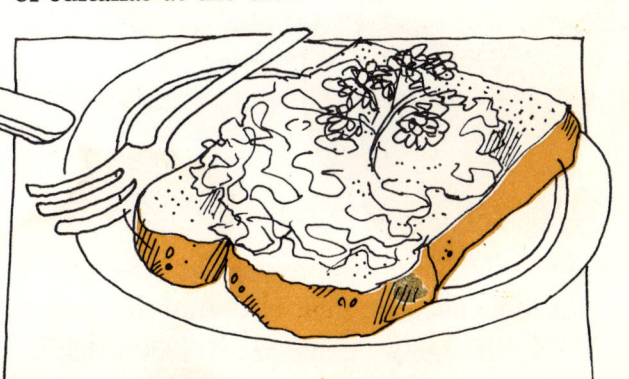

Turn on to a plate or on to a slice of hot buttered toast. Eat at once.

Hot chocolate

This makes a mugful.

Put a mug of milk into a small saucepan. Break in 2 or 3 squares of chocolate.

Put the pan on a very low heat and stir until the milk starts to froth. Watch it or it will boil over.

Pour the chocolate milk back into the mug and put in a large spoon of ice cream if you like.

Don't stir it – the chocolate tastes good through the cold ice cream.

Icy granita

For 2 or 3 glassfuls you will need
- a tray of ice cubes
- a cup of juicy fruit – like canned pineapple pieces, watermelon chunks, strawberries or raspberries

Crush the ice cubes – in a plastic bag banged with a rolling pin maybe.

Mash the fruit in a large bowl and pour in the crushed ice.

Dip in the glasses to fill them.